*To Joe Germain*

# Jungle Animals

By Edward R. Ricciuti
Illustrated by Philip Rymer

## MERRIGOLD PRESS · NEW YORK

# Contents

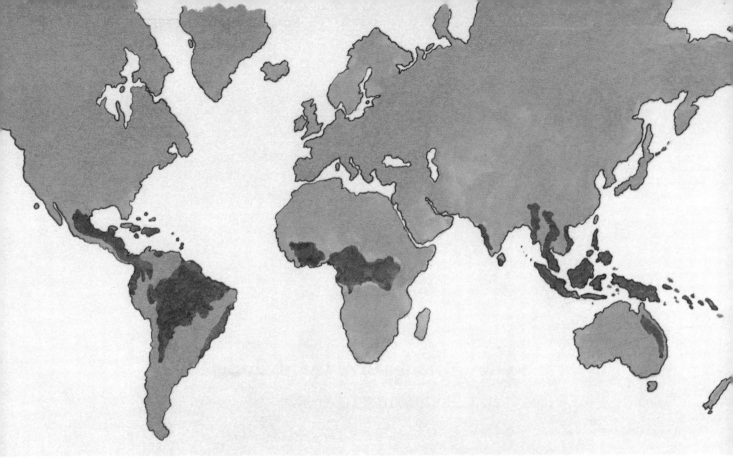

# What Are Jungles?

Jungles are the biggest forests in the world. Many of the plants that grow in them are big, too. Some jungle trees are more than half as tall as the Statue of Liberty. Some vines grow thicker than a person's arm and as long as a jumbo jet.

Many different animals live in jungles. Some are strange, even scary. Tigers, leopards, poisonous frogs, and flying lizards are jungle animals. Gorillas and elephants live in jungles. So do snakes as long as a school bus. Such creatures make jungles seem mysterious and exciting.

Only certain parts of the world have jungles. In the jungle it is like summer all the time. There is lots of rain, too. Some jungles get so much rain they are called rain forests.

# Jungle Trees

There are more kinds of trees in jungles than in other forests. Some jungles have 200 different kinds of trees. A person may have to walk a long way to see the same kind of tree twice.

The tallest jungle trees are more than 200 feet high. Their lowest branches are about 50 feet above the ground.

These giant trees are far apart. They poke above the smaller trees like skyscrapers over a city. Below them are other trees, 40 to 100 feet high. These middle-sized trees grow close together. Many of their branches touch.

The branches and leaves of the middle-sized trees make a green roof, or canopy, over the rest of the jungle. The canopy is so thick that people flying above it in an airplane only see through it once in a while.

The canopy of trees keeps heat in and cool winds out of the jungle. The weather under the canopy almost always stays the same. It is warm but never very hot. Summer in New York City or Chicago can be hotter than in the jungle. The reason is that the canopy keeps out the sun. Because of the shade, the jungle under the canopy never dries out after a rain. The jungle is always damp.

People sometimes think the ground of the jungle is covered with a tangle of vines and bushes. But is is not that way at all. Most plants on the floor of the jungle are small. They do not get enough sun to grow very big.

The only place where vines and other plants do grow thickly in the jungle is where sunshine gets through the canopy. This happens when fire burns trees, wind knocks them down, or people cut them, or where rivers flow through the jungle.

# Vines and Stranglers

The canopy is not made just of the leaves and branches of trees. It is made also of vines and other plants that grow on the trees.

Huge vines called lianas wind through the branches of the canopy. Some lianas grow longer than the tallest trees in the world. They may be hundreds of feet from end to end. Often they have large, green leaves.

A liana begins as a small plant on the ground. It climbs to reach sunlight. It climbs step by step. After it reaches the canopy, it quickly grows bigger.

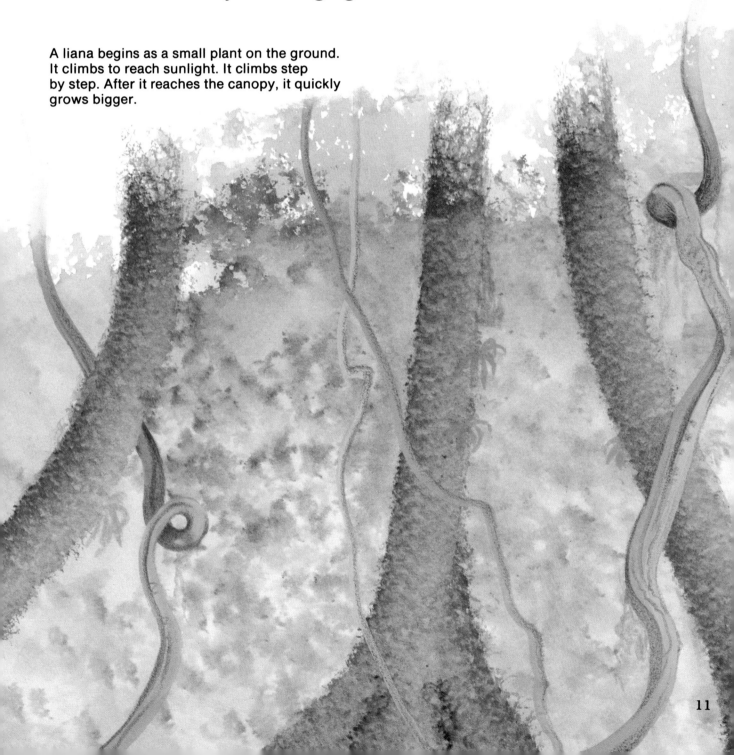

The strangler fig begins as a little bush on a branch. Soon it sends roots down toward the ground.

Another kind of jungle plant that grows on trees is the strangler fig. The name sounds dangerous. But people have nothing to fear from this strangler. It only strangles trees.

The strangler fig does not climb from the ground. It starts in the canopy as a seed. Birds and other animals eat the fig's fruit. Sometimes they drop seeds from the fruit onto tree branches. If a seed stays there it may sprout. Soon the young strangler fig looks like a little bush sitting on a branch.

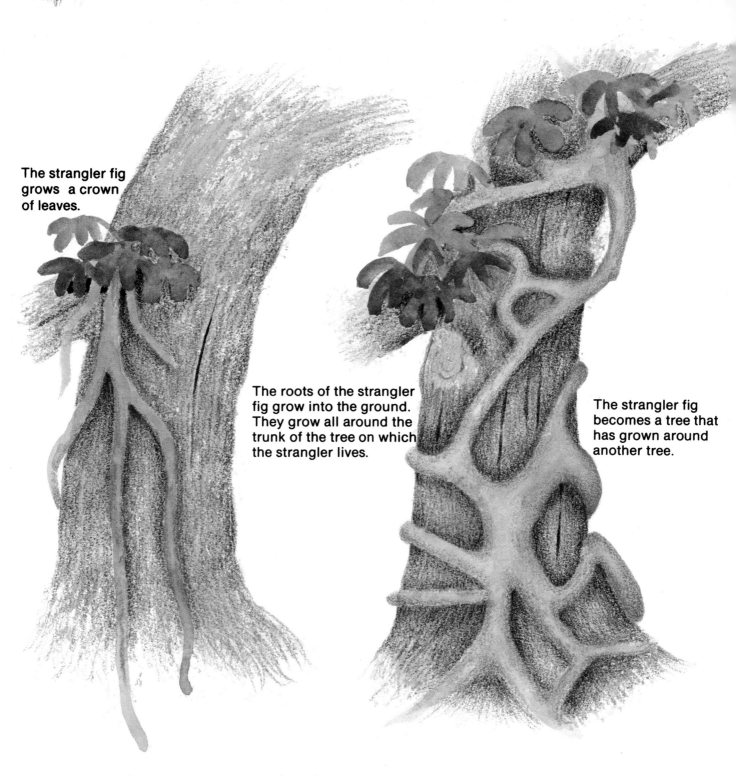

The strangler fig grows a crown of leaves.

The roots of the strangler fig grow into the ground. They grow all around the trunk of the tree on which the strangler lives.

The strangler fig becomes a tree that has grown around another tree.

The young strangler fig sends down roots. Some roots hang in the air. Others creep down the tree trunk. Sooner or later they reach the ground and grow down into it. The roots get thicker as they grow. Finally, they grow all around the tree trunk and hide it from sight.

The tree inside the strangler fig often dies. But its rotting trunk may last hundreds of years. During that time the strangler becomes huge. Some stranglers are so large that a big house with a yard could easily fit inside them.

# Air Plants

When the strangler fig is young and sits on a branch, it is called an air plant. An air plant is any kind of plant that grows on trees and does not touch the ground. More than a hundred different kinds of air plants can grow on one tree.

Air plants do not grow on air. They stick to the bark of a tree. Sometimes they grow in soil that forms in holes and cracks in the trees. Fallen leaves, broken twigs, and droppings from animals pile up in such places. They rot and turn into soil.

Like all plants, air plants need water to live. Some air plants have leaves like bowls where rainwater gathers. Other air plants have roots that take water from the air.

orchids

orchid

fern

Most air plants are related to plants that grow on the ground. Many air plants are orchids. Some of them have beautiful flowers.

Ferns can be air plants, too. They look like the ferns that live on the ground. But they are on trees.

Some air plants have leaves longer than a Ping-Pong table. Other air plants are as big around as an automobile tire. But some of them are as small as the period at the end of this sentence.

The top of the canopy is like the surface of the sea. It is tossed by the wind, pounded by the rain, and baked by the sun. The jungle below the canopy is like the water under the ocean waves. It is always calm and quiet.

Plants that live atop the canopy must be able to stand the wind, the rain, and the heat of the sun. Many of the plants on top have leaves with a skin that is as thick and tough as leather. When raindrops hit them the water slides off without hurting them. Wind does not tear them. And the tough skin protects the soft insides of the leaves from the sun.

If the rain did not hit the canopy first, it would hurt the tender plants below. If the sunshine got through, it would dry them up.

The Puerto Rican parrot nests in holes in trees. On the treeless plains, the parrot would have no place to nest.

The tapir's spreading foot helps it walk on the soft forest floor.

The bushmaster is hard to see in the shadows and leaves of the jungle floor.

# Jungle Animals

Jungles in different parts of the world have many different kinds of animals. Bushbucks, gorillas, forest hogs, and gray parrots live in African jungles. Asian jungles are the home of tigers, gibbon apes, tapirs, and flying frogs. South American jungles have jaguars, sloths, and macaws.

The sloth can travel in the trees, but it can hardly walk on the ground.

The gorilla eats soft forest plants. On the plains, there is only tough grass which the gorilla cannot eat.

Not every kind of animal can live in the jungle. Most animals that live on the plains, away from trees, would find life hard in the jungle. Most jungle animals would find it hard to live on the treeless plains. Each kind of animal in the jungle has special things about it that help it live there.

# Where Some Animals Live in the Jungle

Many animals live in the jungle. Each kind of animal spends most of its time in one part of the jungle. For example, some animals live all their lives in the highest treetops or the middle of the canopy.

Different kinds of animals live in different jungles of the world.

## ANIMALS OF THE SOUTHERN ASIAN JUNGLE

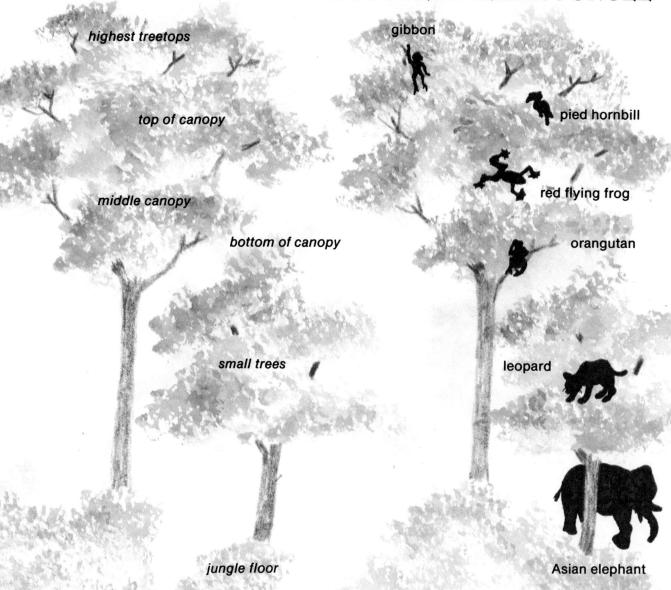

highest treetops

top of canopy

middle canopy

bottom of canopy

small trees

jungle floor

underground

gibbon

pied hornbill

red flying frog

orangutan

leopard

Asian elephant

moles

# ANIMALS OF THE AFRICAN JUNGLE

black and white colobus monkey

giant swallowtail butterfly

gray parrot

pygmy chimpanzee

pangolin

gorilla

earthworms

# ANIMALS OF THE SOUTH AMERICAN JUNGLE

harpy eagle

sloth

squirrel monkey

toucan

boa constrictor

tapir

army ants

21

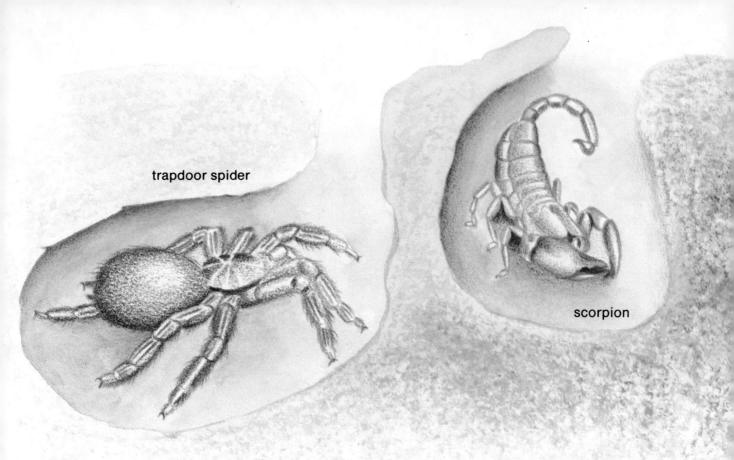

trapdoor spider

scorpion

# Animals That Live Underground

Many animals live in the soil under the jungle floor. Ants and earthworms dig tunnels there. So do beetles and some spiders.

Large animals live in burrows under the jungle floor. In some jungles there are porcupines as big as boxer dogs. They sleep in burrows. Armadillos, which are great diggers, are often jungle animals. Many jungles also have moles, rats, mice, and badgers making burrows in the ground.

Most animals that live under the jungle floor do not dig very deeply. They live within a few feet of the surface. Some, such as moles, spend most of their lives underground. Others come out only at night.

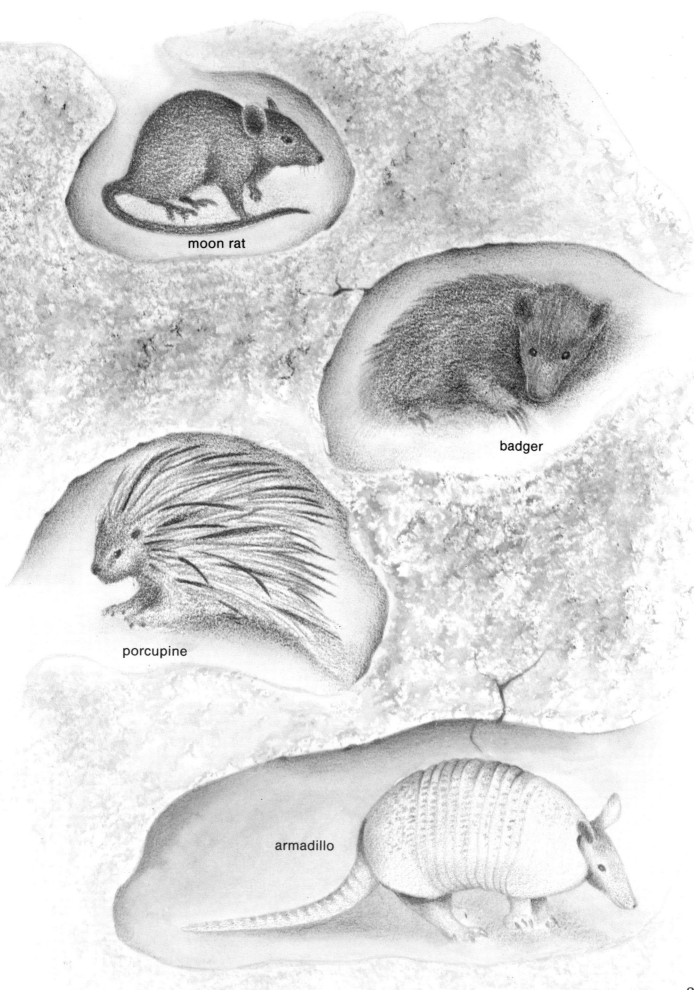

moon rat

badger

porcupine

armadillo

23

tiger

wild pig

# Animals That Live on the Jungle Floor

No thick blanket of leaves covers the ground in the jungle as in some other forests. Leaves that fall off trees rot quickly in the warm, wet jungle. They become part of the soil before they have time to pile up.

The jungle floor is the home of elephants, wild pigs, and pythons—snakes that can be 25 feet long. Buffaloes and big cats such as tigers also live there.

python

elephant

driver ants

Sometimes driver ants march over the jungle floor like armies of tiny soldiers. They have big jaws that are like sharp pincers. A swarm of driver ants can kill a larger animal like a small antelope or pig.

Centipedes also have jaws that are like pincers. Their bite is poisonous. Some have bodies a foot long, with more than 300 legs. They can run fast enough to catch mice and lizards.

Some jungle frogs that live on the jungle floor are poisonous. The poison is in their skin. It protects them from creatures that might try to eat them.

Hunters who live in the same jungles as the poisonous frogs catch and cook them. But the hunters do not eat the frogs. The hunters roast the frogs until the poison drips out of their skin. Then the hunters put the poison on arrows. The poisoned arrows can kill monkeys and birds almost instantly. For this reason the hunters call the frogs arrow-poison frogs.

chameleon

jaguar

boa constrictor

# Where Are the Animals?

Animals are hard to see in jungles. Most jungle creatures are small. Many live in the canopy, out of sight. Even large animals that live on the ground hide easily in the shadows. A jungle can seem empty even though there are animals all around.

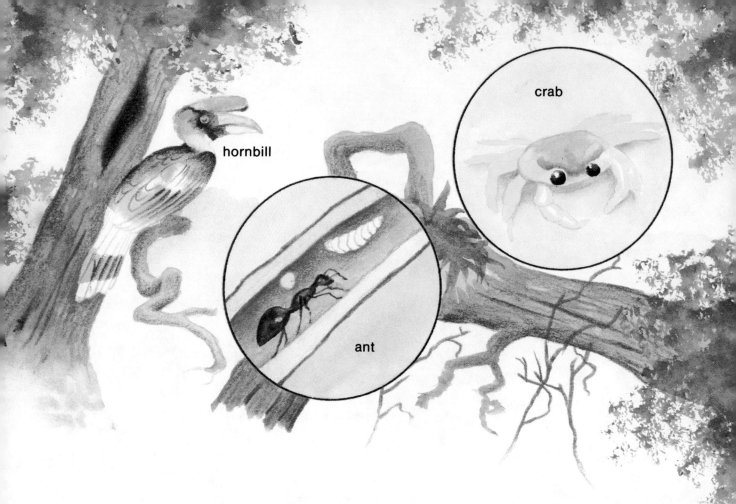

hornbill

crab

ant

# Animals That Live in the Canopy

Some jungle animals such as elephants spend all their lives on the ground. Others—such as jaguars and leopards —live mostly on the ground, but also climb into the trees. Many animals spend all their lives in the canopy. They eat, sleep, mate, and die there.

Almost every part of the canopy is a home for some animal. Birds such as hornbills nest in holes in trees. Birds like bulbuls make nests of leaves and moss in the branches.

The hollow stems of some canopy plants are the homes of ants. Worms and crabs live in the pools of water that form in air plants. Mosquitoes lay their eggs in these pools. So do some frogs. The frogs' eggs hatch into tadpoles, which swim in the pools.

Another kind of frog, the flying frog, lays its eggs on a leaf. When the tadpoles hatch they fall straight down. If they landed on the ground they would die. But they do not land on the ground. They fall into water.

Flying frogs always lay their eggs on a leaf above a small pool of water. The pool is often no bigger than a dinner plate. But the frog puts its eggs in exactly the right spot above it.

Flying frogs have wide feet with webs of skin between their toes. When a flying frog jumps from a branch, it spreads its toes so the webs stretch out. The webs are like parachutes. Instead of crashing down, the frog lands gently.

flying frog

Colobus monkeys have another kind of parachute—very long fur. They often climb very high into the trees. When they jump back down their fur spreads out and keeps them from falling too fast.

A flying lemur has a cape of skin around its body. The cape is attached to its sides, legs, and tail. When the flying lemur jumps from branch to branch it spreads its cape wide. The cape acts almost like wings, letting the lemur glide through the air.

Another animal that acts as if it had wings is the flying lizard. A flying lizard has a flap of very loose skin on each side of its body. It can spread these flaps like fans. Flying lizards can sail through the air as far as 30 feet.

flying lemur

flying lizard

colobus monkey

31

The tree kangaroo is another animal that lives in the canopy. Tree kangaroos are about as big as middle-sized dogs. They have strong hind legs like kangaroos that live on the ground.

A tree kangaroo, pushing off with its legs, can leap 60 feet. The kangaroo uses its long tail to steer in the air.

Tree kangaroos have long, sharp claws that help them climb. There are rough pads on the bottom of the tree kangaroo's feet. The pads help the kangaroo grip tree trunks and branches, and keep the kangaroo from slipping on smooth bark.

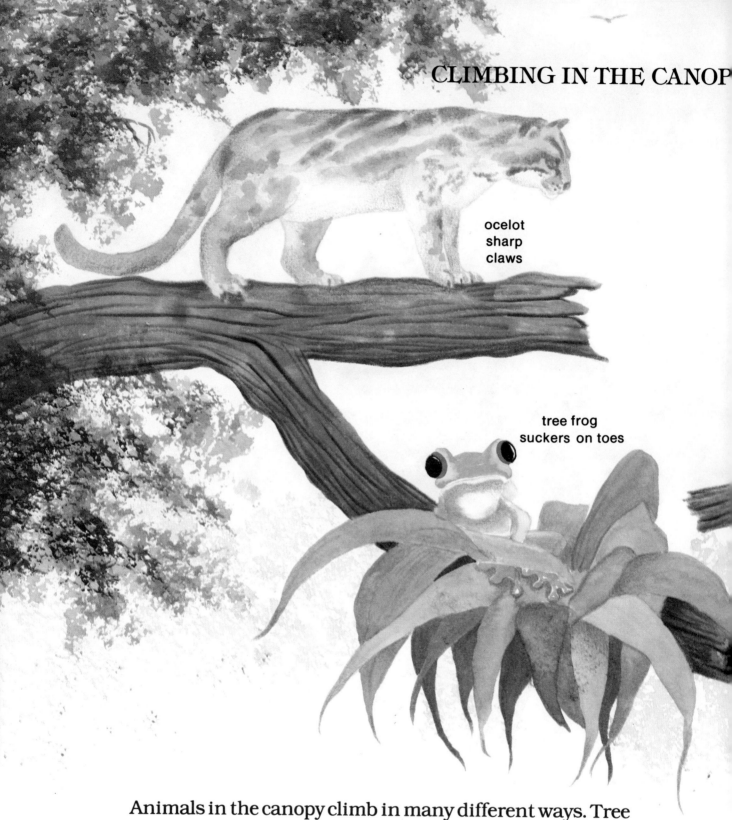

ocelot
sharp
claws

tree frog
suckers on toes

Animals in the canopy climb in many different ways. Tree frogs have tiny suckers on their toes. The suckers stick so tightly they can hold on to wet leaves and slippery bark.

Some monkeys have a tail that acts like an extra hand. It is called a prehensile tail, because it can grasp. The tail can hold on to branches. Spider monkeys and woolly monkeys can hang by their tails. This leaves their hands and feet free for other things.

gibbon
hand like
a hook

anteater
grasping tail

woolly monkey
grasping tail

In some jungles there are also tree porcupines, opossums, and anteaters that can hold on to branches with their tails. When an anteater is attacked by an enemy, it stands on its rear feet with its tail wrapped around a branch. The tail keeps the anteater from falling while it fights with its forefeet. The forefeet are good weapons because they have large, hooked claws.

**Sloths almost never see the world right side up.**

Sloths are other animals in the canopy with claws like hooks. All four feet of the sloth have claws. The sloth spends most of its time hanging upside down by its claws.

Sloths usually travel only when they have to. If there are enough leaves to eat nearby, they may stay where they are for days. Sloths look slow but they move fast and can climb like acrobats.

Hanging upside down is not the only strange thing about a sloth. It also looks green. The green color comes from tiny plants that grow in the sloth's long hair. Looking green helps the sloth hide from enemies.

One enemy of the sloth is the harpy eagle. It is a big, strong bird with a sharp beak and sharp claws. The harpy eagle spends much of the day sitting in the highest treetops. From there it watches the canopy below for animals to catch and eat.

The eagle's eyes are so good it can see monkeys and sloths move in the green tangle of the canopy. But if an animal stays still the eagle may not see it. Sloths move around most when they eat during the night. Then the eagles are sleeping.

# Jungle Animals of the Day

The animals that are awake in the jungle during the day are usually different from those that are awake at night. Two different groups of animals can live in and use the same part of the jungle.

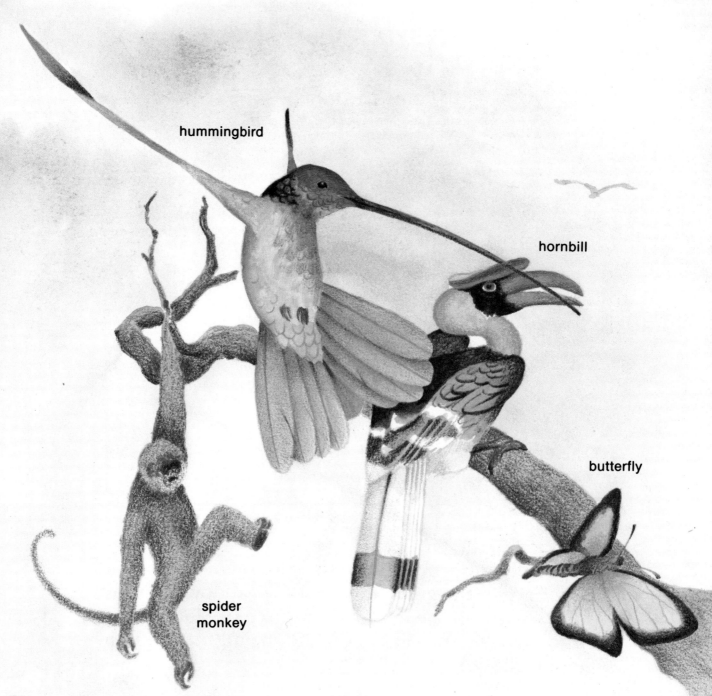

hummingbird

hornbill

butterfly

spider monkey

# Jungle Animals
## of the Night

tree frog

ocelot

owl

bushmaster

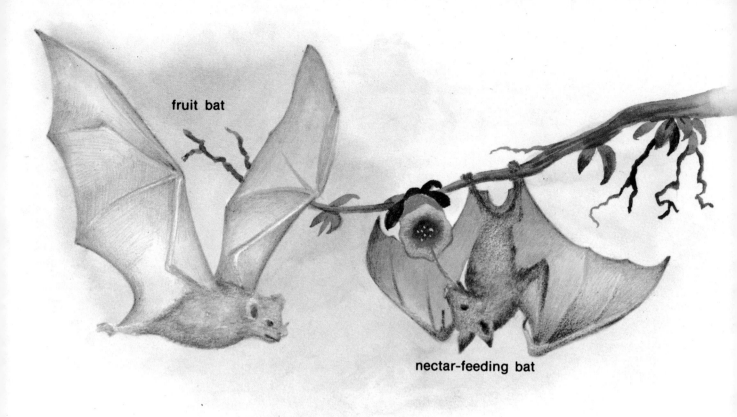

fruit bat

nectar-feeding bat

# Jungle Bats

Jungles have many different kinds of bats. The nectar-feeding bat eats nectar from flowers. Fruit bats eat the juice of fruits and are the biggest bats. Some of them measure three, four, or even five feet from wingtip to wingtip.

The vampire bat is small. It gets its name because it laps up the blood of sleeping animals and, sometimes, people. The blood comes from a tiny nick the vampire makes with its sharp little teeth.

The false vampire bat got its name because people used to believe it fed only on blood like the real vampire bat. The false vampire bat creeps up on sleeping birds and kills and eats them. It also eats other bats.

The fishing bat has long, sharp claws. It swoops low over streams and lakes, and catches small fish in its claws.

The bamboo bat is only about as long as a person's index finger. This hairless bat lives in hollow trees.

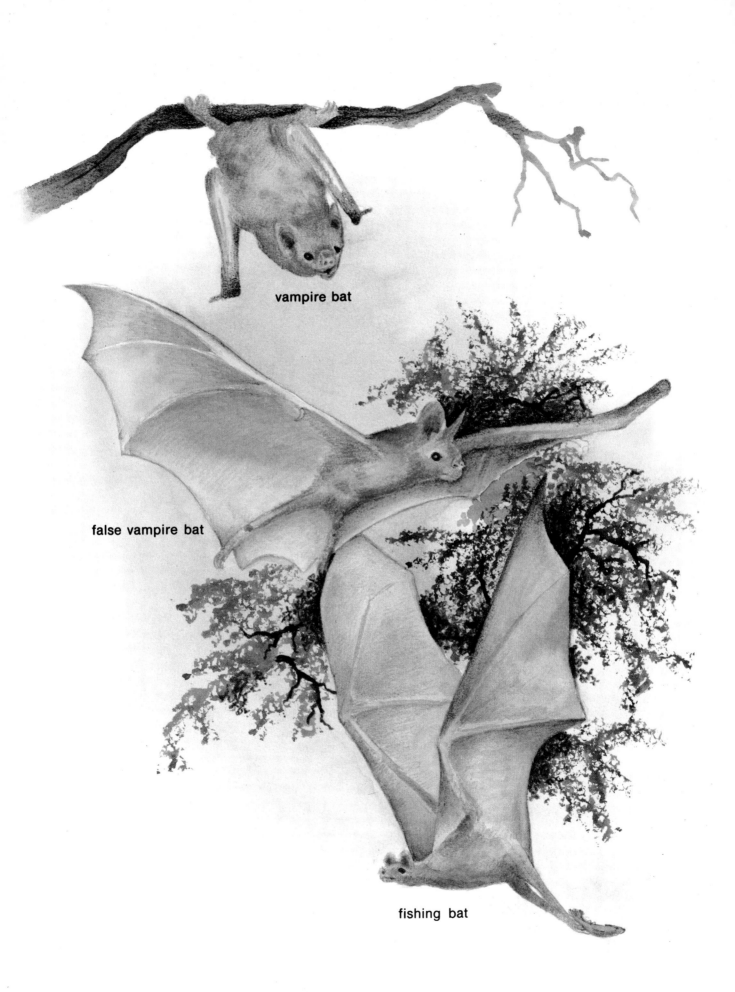

vampire bat

false vampire bat

fishing bat

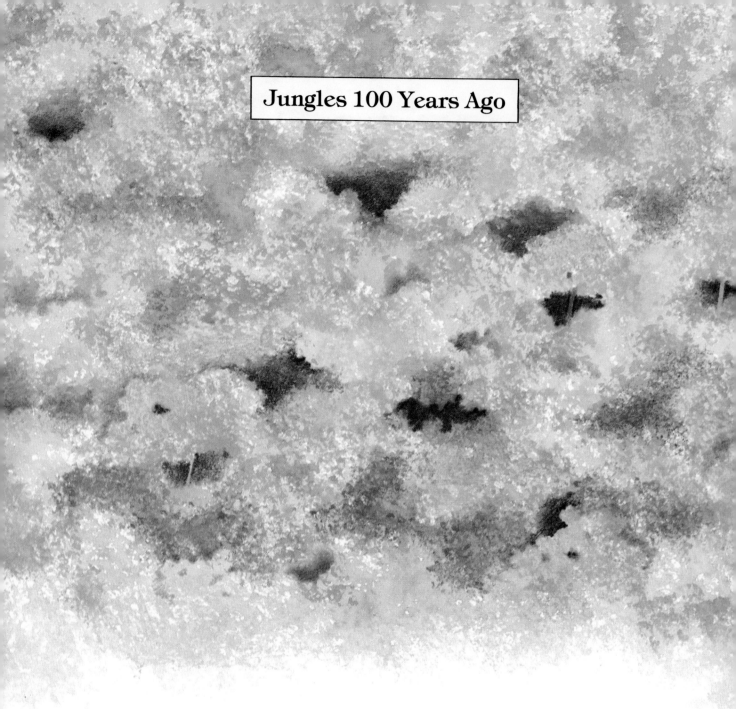

# Disappearing Jungles

Traveling in jungles is a great adventure. Getting to jungles is not as hard as it once was. Good roads lead into many jungles.

Each year, there are more and more people in the world. These people need land on which to live. So they chop down jungles to make room for farms and ranches and factories. They cut down jungle trees to get wood to build houses. Each year, the world has less and less jungle.

# Jungles Now

But the world needs jungles. Without jungles certain kinds of plants would die. Certain kinds of wild animals would die.

There is another important reason why the world needs jungles. Jungles affect the weather and the air that people breathe. No one knows what would happen to the weather and the air if there were no more jungles in the world. For these and other reasons, jungles must not be allowed to disappear.

# Other Books About Jungles

**A book to read now**
Ricciuti, Edward. R. *Plants in Danger*, New York: Harper & Row, Publishers, Inc., 1979.

**More difficult books to read later**
Richards, Paul W. *The Life of the Jungle.* New York: McGraw-Hill Book Company, 1970.

Sanderson, Ivan T. with David Loth. *Ivan Sanderson's Book of Great Jungles.* New York: Simon & Schuster, 1965.

# About the Author and Artist

Edward R. Ricciuti is a well-known and award-winning author of many natural science books for children and adults. While working he has cared for whales on airplane trips, captured sharks, and lived in jungles. He has been a boxer and coach and was a curator at the New York Zoological Society.

Philip Rymer was born in England and used to be a police officer in London. He taught himself to be an artist and has illustrated several books and magazine articles. He is especially interested in birds. Mr. Rymer lives in Texas.

# Index